SPIRALIZER COOKBOOK

MAIN COURSE - 60+ Breakfast, Lunch, Dinner and Dessert Recipes easy to prepare at home

TABLE OF CONTENTS

BREAKFAST 7

SPIRALIZED APPLE PANCAKES 7

SPIRALIZED MELON PANCAKES 9

SPIRALIZED CARROT PANCAKES 10

SPIRALIZED BUTTERNUT SQUASH PANCAKES 11

SPIRALIZED BEET PANCAKES 12

SPIRALIZED ZUCCHINI MUFFINS 13

SPIRALIZED BROCCOLI MUFFINS 15

SPIRALIZED KOHLRABI MUFFINS 17

SPIRALZED CELERIAC MUFFINS 19

SPIRALIZED CARROT MUFFINS 21

SPIRALIED CABBAGE MUFFINS 23

SPIRALIZED CUCUMBER OMELETTE 25

SPIRALIZED ZUCCHINI OMELETTE 27

SPIRALIZED CUCUMBER OMELETTE 29

SPIRALIED RED ONION OMELETTE 31

SPIRALIZED SWEET POTATO OMELETTE 33

SPIRALIZED TORTILLA WITH CHORIZO 35

MEXICAN SHAKSHUKA 36

BRUSSELS SPROTUS AND SWEET POTATO 38

BAKED EGG AND SWEET POTATO 40

LUNCH 42

SPIRALIZED BEETS FRITATTA 42

SPIRALIZED SWEET POTATO FRITATTA 44

SPIRALIED YAMS FRITATTA 46

SPIRALIZED CABBAGE FRITATTA...48

SPIRALIZED CUCUMBER FRITATTA 50

PRAWN SPIRALIZED ROLLS 52

PICKLED CUCUMBERS..54

COCONUT COURGETTE CARPACCIO 55

BLACK BEAN NACHOS...56

WATERCRESS PESTO...57

ZUCCHINI NOODLES SALAD 58

NOODLES SALAD 59

CARROT & GINGER SALAD...60

PASTA SALAD..61

CELERIAC SALAD 62

BUTTERNUT SQUASH SALAD 63

BEET SALAD 64

CUCUMBER SALAD 65

ZUCCHINI NOODLE PASTA SALAD 66

ONION SALAD..67

DINNER..69

SIMPLE PIZZA...69

PEPPERONI PIZZA 71

ZUCCHINI PIZZA 72

BEET PIZZA...73

KALE PIZZA...74

MOZZARELLA PIZZA 76

ZUCCHINI SOUP 77

CUCUMBER SOUP...79

BUTTERNUT SQUASH SOUP 81

CARROT SOUP 83

POTATO SOUP 85

SMOOTHIES.. 88

APPLE SMOOTHIE.. 88

FIBER SMOOTHIE... 89

PEACH SMOOTHIE 90

PINEAPPLE SMOOTHIE 91

KALE SMOOTHIE.. 92

CARROT SMOOTHIE... 93

CHERRY SMOOTHIE 94

AVOCADO SMOOTHIE 95

CRANBERRY SMOOTHIE 96

TROPICAL SMOOTHIE... 97

Associations.

Introduction

Spiralized recipes for personal enjoyment but also for family enjoyment. You will love them for sure for how easy it is to prepare them.

SPIRALIZED APPLE PANCAKES

Serves: **4**

Prep Time: **10**   Minutes

Cook Time: **20**   Minutes

Total Time: **30**   Minutes

INGREDIENTS

- 1 cup whole wheat flour
- ¼ tsp baking soda
- ¼ tsp baking powder
- 1 spiralized apple
- 2 eggs
- 1 cup milk

DIRECTIONS

1. In a bowl combine all ingredients together and mix well
2. In a skillet heat olive oil

3. Pour ¼ of the batter and cook each pancake for 1-2 minutes per side

4. When ready remove from heat and serve

Serves: **4**

Prep Time: **10** Minutes

Cook Time: **30** Minutes

Total Time: **40** Minutes

INGREDIENTS

- 1 cup whole wheat flour
- ¼ tsp baking soda
- ¼ tsp baking powder
- 1 cup spiralized melon
- 2 eggs
- 1 cup milk

DIRECTIONS

1. In a bowl combine all ingredients together and mix well
2. In a skillet heat olive oil
3. Pour ¼ of the batter and cook each pancake for 1-2 minutes per side
4. When ready remove from heat and serve

Serves: **4**

Prep Time: **10**   Minutes

Cook Time: **20**   Minutes

Total Time: **30**   Minutes

INGREDIENTS

- 1 cup whole wheat flour
- ¼ tsp baking soda
- ¼ tsp baking powder
- 1 cup spiralized carrot
- 2 eggs
- 1 cup milk

DIRECTIONS

1. In a bowl combine all ingredients together and mix well
2. In a skillet heat olive oil
3. Pour ¼ of the batter and cook each pancake for 1-2 minutes per side
4. When ready remove from heat and serve

SPIRALIZED BUTTERNUT SQUASH PANCAKES

Serves: **4**
Prep Time: **10** Minutes

Cook Time: **20** Minutes

Total Time: **30** Minutes

INGREDIENTS

- 1 cup whole wheat flour
- ¼ tsp baking soda
- ¼ tsp baking powder
- 1 cup spiralized butternut squash
- 2 eggs
- 1 cup milk

DIRECTIONS

1. In a bowl combine all ingredients together and mix well
2. In a skillet heat olive oil
3. Pour ¼ of the batter and cook each pancake for 1-2 minutes per side
4. When ready remove from heat and serve

Serves: **4**

Prep Time: **10**   Minutes

Cook Time: **30**   Minutes

Total Time: **40**   Minutes

INGREDIENTS

- 1 cup whole wheat flour
- ¼ tsp baking soda
- ¼ tsp baking powder
- 1 cup spiralized beet
- 2 eggs
- 1 cup milk

DIRECTIONS

1. In a bowl combine all ingredients together and mix well
2. In a skillet heat olive oil
3. Pour ¼ of the batter and cook each pancake for 1-2 minutes per side
4. When ready remove from heat and serve

SPIRALIZED ZUCCHINI MUFFINS

Serves: **8-12**
Prep Time: **10**   Minutes
Cook Time: **20**   Minutes
Total Time: **30**   Minutes

INGREDIENTS

- 2 eggs
- 1 tablespoon olive oil
- 1 cup milk
- 2 cups whole wheat flour
- 1 tsp baking soda
- ¼ tsp baking soda
- 1 cup spiralized zucchini
- ¼ cup molasses

DIRECTIONS

1. In a bowl combine all dry ingredients
2. In another bowl combine all dry ingredients
3. Combine wet and dry ingredients together

4. Pour mixture into 8-12 prepared muffin cups, fill 2/3 of the cups

5. Bake for 18-20 minutes at 375 F

6. When ready remove from the oven and serve

Serves:	**8-12**	
Prep Time:	**10**	Minutes
Cook Time:	**20**	Minutes
Total Time:	**30**	Minutes

INGREDIENTS

- 2 eggs
- 1 tablespoon olive oil
- 1 cup milk
- 2 cups whole wheat flour
- 1 tsp baking soda
- ¼ tsp baking soda
- 1 tsp cinnamon
- 1 cup spiralized broccoli

DIRECTIONS

1. In a bowl combine all dry ingredients
2. In another bowl combine all dry ingredients
3. Combine wet and dry ingredients together

4. Pour mixture into 8-12 prepared muffin cups, fill 2/3 of the cups

5. Bake for 18-20 minutes at 375 F

6. When ready remove from the oven and serve

Serves: **8-12**
Prep Time: **10**   Minutes
Cook Time: **20**   Minutes
Total Time: **30**   Minutes

INGREDIENTS

- 2 eggs
- 1 tablespoon olive oil
- 1 cup milk
- 2 cups whole wheat flour
- 1 tsp baking soda
- ¼ tsp baking soda
- 1 tsp cinnamon
- 1 cup spiralized kohlrabi

DIRECTIONS

1. In a bowl combine all dry ingredients
2. In another bowl combine all dry ingredients
3. Combine wet and dry ingredients together

4. Pour mixture into 8-12 prepared muffin cups, fill 2/3 of the cups

5. Bake for 18-20 minutes at 375 F

6. When ready remove from the oven and serve

Serves: **8-12**

Prep Time: **10**   Minutes

Cook Time: **20**   Minutes

Total Time: **30**   Minutes

INGREDIENTS

- 2 eggs
- 1 tablespoon olive oil
- 1 cup milk
- 2 cups whole wheat flour
- 1 tsp baking soda
- ¼ tsp baking soda
- 1 tsp cinnamon
- 1 cup spiralized celeriac

DIRECTIONS

1. In a bowl combine all dry ingredients
2. In another bowl combine all dry ingredients
3. Combine wet and dry ingredients together

4. Pour mixture into 8-12 prepared muffin cups, fill 2/3 of the cups

5. Bake for 18-20 minutes at 375 F

6. When ready remove from the oven and serve

Serves: **8-12**
Prep Time: **10**   Minutes

Cook Time: **20**   Minutes

Total Time: **30**   Minutes

INGREDIENTS

- 2 eggs
- 1 tablespoon olive oil
- 1 cup milk
- 2 cups whole wheat flour
- 1 tsp baking soda
- ¼ tsp baking soda
- 1 tsp cinnamon
- 1 cup spiralized carrot

DIRECTIONS

1. In a bowl combine all dry ingredients
2. In another bowl combine all dry ingredients
3. Combine wet and dry ingredients together

4. Pour mixture into 8-12 prepared muffin cups, fill 2/3 of the cups

5. Bake for 18-20 minutes at 375 F

6. When ready remove from the oven and serve

SPIRALIED CABBAGE MUFFINS

Serves: **8-12**
Prep Time: **10**   Minutes

Cook Time: **20**   Minutes

Total Time: **30**   Minutes

INGREDIENTS

- 2 eggs
- 1 tablespoon olive oil
- 1 cup milk
- 2 cups whole wheat flour
- 1 tsp baking soda
- ¼ tsp baking soda
- 1 tsp spiralized cabbage

DIRECTIONS

1. In a bowl combine all dry ingredients
2. In another bowl combine all dry ingredients
3. Combine wet and dry ingredients together

4. Pour mixture into 8-12 prepared muffin cups, fill 2/3 of the cups

5. Bake for 18-20 minutes at 375 F

6. When ready remove from the oven and serve

Serves: **1**
Prep Time: **5**   Minutes

Cook Time: **10**   Minutes

Total Time: **15**   Minutes

INGREDIENTS

- 2 eggs
- ¼ tsp salt
- ¼ tsp black pepper
- 1 tablespoon olive oil
- 1 cup spiralized cucumber
- ¼ tsp basil

DIRECTIONS

1. In a bowl combine all ingredients together and mix well
2. In a skillet heat olive oil and pour the egg mixture
3. Cook for 1-2 minutes per side

4. When ready remove omelette from the skillet and serve

SPIRALIZED ZUCCHINI OMELETTE

Serves: **1**
Prep Time: **5**   Minutes

Cook Time: **10**   Minutes

Total Time: **15**   Minutes

INGREDIENTS

- 2 eggs
- ¼ tsp salt
- ¼ tsp black pepper
- 1 tablespoon olive oil
- ¼ cup cheese
- ¼ tsp basil
- 1 cup spiralized zucchini

DIRECTIONS

1. In a bowl combine all ingredients together and mix well
2. In a skillet heat olive oil and pour the egg mixture
3. Cook for 1-2 minutes per side

4. When ready remove omelette from the skillet and serve

Serves: *1*
Prep Time: 5   Minutes

Cook Time: *10* Minutes

Total Time: *15* Minutes

INGREDIENTS

- 2 eggs
- ¼ tsp salt
- ¼ tsp black pepper
- 1 tablespoon olive oil
- ¼ cup cheese
- ¼ tsp basil
- 1 cup spiralized cucumber

DIRECTIONS

1. In a bowl combine all ingredients together and mix well
2. In a skillet heat olive oil and pour the egg mixture
3. Cook for 1-2 minutes per side

4. When ready remove omelette from the skillet and
    serve

Serves: **1**

Prep Time: **5** Minutes

Cook Time: **10** Minutes

Total Time: **15** Minutes

INGREDIENTS

- 2 eggs
- ¼ tsp salt
- ¼ tsp black pepper
- 1 tablespoon olive oil
- ¼ cup cheese
- ¼ tsp basil
- 1 cup spiralized red onion

DIRECTIONS

1. In a bowl combine all ingredients together and mix well
2. In a skillet heat olive oil and pour the egg mixture
3. Cook for 1-2 minutes per side

4. When ready remove omelette from the skillet and serve

SPIRALIZED SWEET POTATO OMELETTE

Serves: **1**
Prep Time: **5**   Minutes

Cook Time: **10**   Minutes

Total Time: **15**   Minutes

INGREDIENTS

- 2 eggs
- ¼ tsp salt
- ¼ tsp black pepper
- 1 tablespoon olive oil
- ¼ cup cheese
- ¼ tsp basil
- 1 cup spiralized sweet potato

DIRECTIONS

1. In a bowl combine all ingredients together and mix well
2. In a skillet heat olive oil and pour the egg mixture
3. Cook for 1-2 minutes per side

4. When ready remove omelette from the skillet and serve

Serves: *1*
Prep Time: 5   Minutes

Cook Time: *15*   Minutes

Total Time: *20*   Minutes

INGREDIENTS

- 1 tablespoon olive oil
- 1 red onion
- 2 chorizo links
- 1 lb. sweet potatoes
- 6 eggs
- 1 tablespoon parsley

DIRECTIONS

1. In a skillet heat olive oil, add onion, chorizo, potato noodles and cook for 5-10 minutes
2. Add eggs, parsley and cook for another 3-4 minutes
3. When ready transfer to a plate and serve

Serves: *2*

Prep Time: *10* Minutes

Cook Time: *25* Minutes

Total Time: *35* Minutes

INGREDIENTS

- 1 tablespoon olive oil
- 1 sweet potato
- 2 cups tomato puree
- 2 garlic cloves
- 1 tsp chili powder
- ¼ tsp cumin
- 2 eggs
- 1 avocado
- 1 tablespoon cilantro

DIRECTIONS

1. In a skillet heat olive oil and add potato noodles
2. Cook for 5-10 minutes

3. Add cilantro, garlic clove, chili powder, tomato pure and cumin

4. Cook for another 5-10 minutes

5. Crack the eggs over the mixture and bake everything at 400 F for 12-15 minutes

6. When ready remove from the oven and serve

Serves: *2*

Prep Time: *10* Minutes

Cook Time: *35* Minutes

Total Time: *45* Minutes

INGREDIENTS

- 1 lb. brussels sprouts
- 1 butternut squash
- 1 tablespoon olive oil
- 1 tsp garlic powder
- 4-5 strips bacon
- 3-4 eggs

DIRECTIONS

1. Place the butternut squash noodles and brussels sprouts in a baking dish and drizzle olive oil over

2. Add garlic powder, bacon bites, and bake at 375 F for 20-25 minutes

3. Crack the eggs over the noodles and cook for another 5-10 minutes

4. When ready remove from the oven and serve

BAKED EGG AND SWEET POTATO

Serves: **2**

Prep Time: **10**   Minutes

Cook Time: **20**   Minutes

Total Time: **30**   Minutes

INGREDIENTS

- 1 sweet potato
- 1 tablespoon olive oil
- 2 eggs
- ¼ tsp salt
- ¼ tsp black pepper

DIRECTIONS

1. Spiralize your vegetables and place them on a baking sheet
2. Add the remaining ingredients
3. Crack the eggs over the noodles
4. Bake at 400 F for 18-20 minutes
5. When ready remove from the oven and serve

SPIRALIZED BEETS FRITATTA

Serves: *2*
Prep Time: *10*   Minutes

Cook Time: *20*   Minutes

Total Time: *30*   Minutes

INGREDIENTS

- 1 cup spiralized beets
- 1 tablespoon olive oil
- ½ red onion
- ¼ tsp salt
- 2 oz. cheddar cheese
- 1 garlic clove
- ¼ tsp dill

DIRECTIONS

1. In a bowl whisk eggs with salt and cheese
2. In a frying pan heat olive oil and pour egg mixture

3. Add remaining ingredients and mix well
4. Serve when ready

Serves: **2**
Prep Time: **10**   Minutes

Cook Time: **20**   Minutes

Total Time: **30**   Minutes

INGREDIENTS

- **1 cup spiralized sweet potato**
- **1 tablespoon olive oil**
- **½ red onion**
- **¼ tsp salt**
- **2 oz. cheddar cheese**
- **1 garlic clove**
- **¼ tsp dill**

DIRECTIONS

1. **In a bowl whisk eggs with salt and cheese**
2. **In a frying pan heat olive oil and pour egg mixture**
3. **Add remaining ingredients and mix well**

4. Serve when ready

Serves: **2**

Prep Time: **10** Minutes

Cook Time: **20** Minutes

Total Time: **30** Minutes

INGREDIENTS

- 1 cup spiralized yams
- 1 tablespoon olive oil
- ½ red onion
- ¼ tsp salt
- 2 oz. cheddar cheese
- 1 garlic clove
- ¼ tsp dill

DIRECTIONS

1. In a bowl whisk eggs with salt and cheese
2. In a frying pan heat olive oil and pour egg mixture
3. Add remaining ingredients and mix well

4. Serve when ready

Serves: **2**

Prep Time: **10** Minutes

Cook Time: **20** Minutes

Total Time: **30** Minutes

INGREDIENTS

- 1 cup spiralized cabbage
- 1 tablespoon olive oil
- ½ red onion
- ¼ tsp salt
- 2 oz. parmesan cheese
- 1 garlic clove
- ¼ tsp dill

DIRECTIONS

1. In a bowl whisk eggs with salt and parmesan cheese
2. In a frying pan heat olive oil and pour egg mixture
3. Add remaining ingredients and mix well

4. Serve when ready

SPIRALIZED CUCUMBER FRITATTA

Serves: **2**

Prep Time: **10**   Minutes

Cook Time: **20**   Minutes

Total Time: **30**   Minutes

INGREDIENTS

- **1 cup spiralized cucumber**
- **1 tablespoon olive oil**
- **½ red onion**
- **¼ tsp salt**
- **2 oz. cheddar cheese**
- **1 garlic clove**
- **¼ tsp dill**

DIRECTIONS

1. **In a bowl whisk eggs with salt and cheese**
2. **In a frying pan heat olive oil and pour egg mixture**
3. **Add remaining ingredients and mix well**

4. Serve when ready

Serves: **4**

Prep Time: **5**   Minutes

Cook Time: **10**   Minutes

Total Time: **15**   Minutes

INGREDIENTS

- 4 rice paper wrappers
- ¼ pack coriander
- ¼ pack mint
- 8-10 prawns
- 1 carrot
- 1 courgette
- Dipping sauce

DIRECTIONS

1. Dip a rice paper wrapper into water
2. Place coriander leaves over, add prawns, spiralized veggies and remaining ingredients
3. Fold the sides of the wrapper into the center, over the filling

4. Serve when ready with sauce

Serves: **1**

Prep Time: **5**   Minutes

Cook Time: **10** Minutes

Total Time: **15** Minutes

INGREDIENTS

- 1 cucumber
- 1 tsp salt
- 1 tablespoon wine vinegar
- 1 tsp sugar
- ¼ tsp coriander seeds
- 1 handful of dill

DIRECTIONS

1. **In a bowl combine all ingredients together with spiralized cucumber and serve**

Serves: **1**

Prep Time: **5**   Minutes

Cook Time: **5**   Minutes

Total Time: **10**   Minutes

INGREDIENTS

- ½ lb. edamame beans
- 1 tablespoon olive oil
- Juice of ½ lime
- 2 courgettes
- 1 pack radishes

DIRECTIONS

1. In a saucepan bring water to a boil and cook edamame beans for 4-5 minutes
2. In a bowl combine olive oil and lime juice together
3. Lay the courgette ribbons on a plate and scatter over the edamame beans, radishes and dressing
4. Serve when ready

Serves: *2*

Prep Time: *10*   Minutes

Cook Time: *20*   Minutes

Total Time: *30*   Minutes

INGREDIENTS

- 2 lb. potatoes
- 1 tablespoon olive oil
- ½ lb. cheddar cheese
- 1 lb. black beans
- 1 pack coriander
- red pepper salsa

DIRECTIONS

1. Cut the potatoes into thin slices
2. Bake the potatoes at 350 F for 12-15 minutes
3. Add in layers cheese, beans and remaining ingredients
4. When ready remove from the oven and serve with red pepper salsa

Serves: **1**

Prep Time: **5** Minutes

Cook Time: **5** Minutes

Total Time: **10** Minutes

INGREDIENTS

- ½ lb. watercress
- 1 garlic clove
- 2 oz. nuts
- Juice from 1 lemon
- 1 oz. parmesan cheese
- 1 tablespoon olive oil

DIRECTIONS

1. Place all ingredients in a blender
2. Blend until smooth
3. When ready remove pesto from the blender and serve

ZUCCHINI NOODLES SALAD

Serves: *1*
Prep Time: *5*   Minutes

Cook Time: *5*   Minutes

Total Time: *10* Minutes

INGREDIENTS

- 2 spiralized zucchinis
- 1 clove garlic
- ½ cup parmesan cheese
- 1 cup pesto

DIRECTIONS

1. In a bowl mix all ingredients and mix well
2. Serve with dressing

Serves: *1*
Prep Time: 5   Minutes

Cook Time: 5   Minutes

Total Time: *10*   Minutes

INGREDIENTS

- 1 spiralized zucchini
- 1 spiralized carrot
- ¼ cup honey
- ¼ cup pecans
- 1 cup salad dressing

DIRECTIONS

1. In a bowl mix all ingredients and mix well
2. Serve with dressing

Serves: *1*
Prep Time: *5*   Minutes

Cook Time: *5*   Minutes

Total Time: *10*   Minutes

INGREDIENTS

- 4 spiralized carrots
- ¼ cup honey
- ¼ cup pecans
- 1 cup salad dressing
- 1 tsp ginger

DIRECTIONS

1. In a bowl mix all ingredients and mix well
2. Serve with dressing

PASTA SALAD

Serves: *1*
Prep Time: *5*   Minutes

Cook Time: *5*   Minutes

Total Time: *10*   Minutes

INGREDIENTS

- 2 tablespoons wine vinegar
- 1 tsp oregano
- 1 red spiralized onion
- 1 spiralized cucumber
- 1 spiralized cabbage
- 1 cup salad dressing

DIRECTIONS

1. a bowl mix all ingredients and mix well
2. Serve with dressing

Serves: *1*
Prep Time: *5*   Minutes

Cook Time: *5*   Minutes

Total Time: *10*   Minutes

INGREDIENTS

- 2 spiralized carrots
- 2 spiralized celeriac bulb
- 1 tsp mustard
- 1 tsp apple cider vinegar
- 1 tsp salt

DIRECTIONS

1. In a bowl mix all ingredients and mix well
2. Serve with dressing

BUTTERNUT SQUASH SALAD

Serves: *1*
Prep Time: *5*   Minutes

Cook Time: *5*   Minutes

Total Time: *10* Minutes

INGREDIENTS

- 1 tablespoon honey
- 1 spiralized butternut squash
- 2 tomatoes
- 1 cup greens
- 1 cup salad dressing

DIRECTIONS

1. In a bowl mix all ingredients and mix well
2. Serve with dressing

Serves: *1*
Prep Time: *5*   Minutes

Cook Time: *5*   Minutes

Total Time: *10* Minutes

INGREDIENTS

- 1 cup arugula leaves
- 2 spiralized beets
- ¼ cup pecans
- 1 cup salad dressing

DIRECTIONS

1. In a bowl mix all ingredients and mix well
2. Serve with dressing

CUCUMBER SALAD

Serves: **1**
Prep Time: **5**   Minutes

Cook Time: **5**   Minutes

Total Time: **10** Minutes

INGREDIENTS

- 1 spiralized cucumber
- 2 tomatoes
- 1 tsp mustard
- 1 cup salad dressing

DIRECTIONS

1. In a bowl mix all ingredients and mix well
2. Serve with dressing

ZUCCHINI NOODLE PASTA SALAD

Serves: **1**

Prep Time: **5**   Minutes

Cook Time: **5**   Minutes

Total Time: **10**   Minutes

INGREDIENTS

- 1 ear corn
- 1 tablespoon olive oil
- 2 spiralized zucchini
- 1 cup feta cheese

DIRECTIONS

1. In a bowl mix all ingredients and mix well
2. Serve with dressing

Serves: *1*
Prep Time: *5*   Minutes

Cook Time: *5*   Minutes

Total Time: *10*   Minutes

INGREDIENTS

- 1 spiralized onion
- 1 spiralized zucchini
- 1 spiralized cucumber
- 1 tomato
- 4 oz. feta cheese

DIRECTIONS

1. In a bowl mix all ingredients and mix well
2. Serve with dressing

SIMPLE PIZZA

Serves: **6-8**
Prep Time: **10**   Minutes

Cook Time: **15**   Minutes

Total Time: **25**   Minutes

INGREDIENTS

- 1 pizza spiralized sweet potato crust
- ½ cup tomato sauce
- ¼ black pepper
- 1 cup pepperoni slices
- 1 cup mozzarella
- 1 cup olives

DIRECTIONS

1. Spiralized the tomato and shape it like a crust
2. Spread tomato sauce on the pizza crust
3. Place all the toppings on the pizza crust

4. Bake the pizza at 425 F for 12-15 minutes

5. When ready remove pizza from the oven and serve

Serves: **6-8**
Prep Time: **10**   Minutes

Cook Time: **15**   Minutes

Total Time: **25**   Minutes

INGREDIENTS

- 1 pizza spiralized sweet potato crust
- 1 cup pepperoni slices
- 1 cup mushrooms
- 1 cup red bell pepper
- ½ cup tomato sauce

DIRECTIONS

1. Spiralized the tomato and shape it like a crust
2. Spread tomato sauce on the pizza crust
3. Place all the toppings on the pizza crust
4. Bake the pizza at 425 F for 12-15 minutes
5. When ready remove pizza from the oven and serve

Serves: **6-8**
Prep Time: **10**   Minutes

Cook Time: **15**   Minutes

Total Time: **25**   Minutes

INGREDIENTS

- 1 pizza spiralized sweet potato crust
- ½ cup tomato sauce
- 1 cup olives
- 1 cup spiralized zucchini
- 1 cup salami

DIRECTIONS

1. Spiralized the tomato and shape it like a crust
2. Spread tomato sauce on the pizza crust
3. Place all the toppings on the pizza crust
4. Bake the pizza at 425 F for 12-15 minutes
5. When ready remove pizza from the oven and serve

BEET PIZZA

Serves: **6-8**

Prep Time: **10**   Minutes

Cook Time: **15**   Minutes

Total Time: **25**   Minutes

INGREDIENTS

- 1 pizza spiralized sweet potato crust
- ½ cup tomato sauce
- 1 cup spiralized beet
- 1 cup mozzarella cheese
- 1 cup black olives

DIRECTIONS

1. Spiralized the tomato and shape it like a crust
2. Spread tomato sauce on the pizza crust
3. Place all the toppings on the pizza crust
4. Bake the pizza at 425 F for 12-15 minutes
5. When ready remove pizza from the oven and serve

Serves: **6-8**
Prep Time: **10**   Minutes

Cook Time: **15**   Minutes

Total Time: **25**   Minutes

INGREDIENTS

- 1 pizza spiralized sweet potato crust
- ½ cup tomato sauce
- 1 cup kale
- 1 cup salami
- 1 cup mozzarella cheese

DIRECTIONS

1. Spiralized the tomato and shape it like a crust
2. Spread tomato sauce on the pizza crust
3. Place all the toppings on the pizza crust
4. Bake the pizza at 425 F for 12-15 minutes

5. When ready remove pizza from the oven and serve

Serves: **6-8**
Prep Time: **10**   Minutes

Cook Time: **15**   Minutes

Total Time: **25**   Minutes

INGREDIENTS

- 1 pizza spiralized sweet potato crust
- ½ cup tomato sauce
- 1 cup mozzarella
- ½ cup parmesan
- 1 cup gorgonzola

DIRECTIONS

1. Spiralized the tomato and shape it like a crust
2. Spread tomato sauce on the pizza crust
3. Place all the toppings on the pizza crust
4. Bake the pizza at 425 F for 12-15 minutes
5. When ready remove pizza from the oven and serve

Serves: *4*

Prep Time: *10*   Minutes

Cook Time: *20*   Minutes

Total Time: *30*   Minutes

INGREDIENTS

- 1 tablespoon olive oil
- 1 lb. spiralized zucchini
- ¼ red onion
- ½ cup all-purpose flour
- ¼ tsp salt
- ¼ tsp pepper
- 1 can vegetable broth
- 1 cup heavy cream

DIRECTIONS

1. In a saucepan heat olive oil and sauté spiralized zucchini until tender
2. Add remaining ingredients to the saucepan and bring to a boil

3. When ready pour soup into bowls,
4. Garnish with parsley and serve

Serves: **4**

Prep Time: **10** Minutes

Cook Time: **20** Minutes

Total Time: **30** Minutes

INGREDIENTS

- 1 tablespoon olive oil
- 1 lb. spiralized cucumber
- ¼ red onion
- ½ cup all-purpose flour
- ¼ tsp salt
- ¼ tsp pepper
- 1 can vegetable broth
- 1 cup heavy cream

DIRECTIONS

1. In a saucepan heat olive oil and sauté cucumber until tender
2. Add remaining ingredients to the saucepan and bring to a boil

3. When ready pour soup into bowls,
4. Garnish with parsley and serve

BUTTERNUT SQUASH SOUP

Serves: **4**

Prep Time: **10** Minutes

Cook Time: **20** Minutes

Total Time: **30** Minutes

INGREDIENTS

- 1 tablespoon olive oil
- 1 lb. spiralized butternut squash
- ¼ red onion
- ½ cup all-purpose flour
- ¼ tsp salt
- ¼ tsp pepper
- 1 can vegetable broth
- 1 cup heavy cream

DIRECTIONS

1. In a saucepan heat olive oil and sauté butternut until tender
2. Add remaining ingredients to the saucepan and bring to a boil

3. When ready pour soup into bowls,
4. Garnish with parsley and serve

Serves: **4**

Prep Time: **10**   Minutes

Cook Time: **20**   Minutes

Total Time: **30**   Minutes

INGREDIENTS

- 1 tablespoon olive oil
- 1 lb. spiralized carrot
- ¼ red onion
- ½ cup all-purpose flour
- ¼ tsp salt
- ¼ tsp pepper
- 1 can vegetable broth
- 1 cup heavy cream

DIRECTIONS

1. In a saucepan heat olive oil and sauté carrots until tender

2. Add remaining ingredients to the saucepan and bring to a boil

3. When ready pour soup into bowls,

4. Garnish with parsley and serve

Serves: **4**

Prep Time: **10**   Minutes

Cook Time: **20**   Minutes

Total Time: **30**   Minutes

INGREDIENTS

- 1 tablespoon olive oil
- 1 lb. spiralized potato
- ¼ red onion
- ½ cup all-purpose flour
- ¼ tsp salt
- ¼ tsp pepper
- 1 can vegetable broth
- 1 cup heavy cream

DIRECTIONS

1. In a saucepan heat olive oil and sauté potatoes until tender
2. Add remaining ingredients to the saucepan and bring to a boil

3. When ready pour soup into bowls,
4. Garnish with parsley and serve

SMOOTHIES

APPLE SMOOTHIE

Serves: **1**

Prep Time: **5**   Minutes

Cook Time: **5**   Minutes

Total Time: **10**   Minutes

INGREDIENTS

- 1 cup apple
- 1 cup spinach
- 1 pinch cinnamon
- 1 cup coconut water

DIRECTIONS

1. In a blender place all ingredients and blend until smooth
2. Pour smoothie in a glass and serve

FIBER SMOOTHIE

Serves: *1*
Prep Time: 5   Minutes

Cook Time: 5   Minutes

Total Time: *10* Minutes

INGREDIENTS

- 1 cup blueberries
- 1 banana
- 1 cup spinach
- 1 cup Greek yogurt
- 1 tablespoon honey

DIRECTIONS

1. In a blender place all ingredients and blend until smooth
2. Pour smoothie in a glass and serve

PEACH SMOOTHIE

Serves: *1*
Prep Time: *5*   Minutes

Cook Time: *5*   Minutes

Total Time: *10*   Minutes

INGREDIENTS

- 2 peaches
- 1 cup coconut water
- 1 tsp honey
- 1 tsp brown sugar
- 1 cup ice
- 1 banana

DIRECTIONS

1. **In a blender place all ingredients and blend until smooth**
2. **Pour smoothie in a glass and serve**

PINEAPPLE SMOOTHIE

Serves: **1**

Prep Time: **5**   Minutes

Cook Time: **5**   Minutes

Total Time: **10** Minutes

INGREDIENTS

- 1 cup pineapple
- 1 cup strawberries
- 1 cup kale
- 2 tablespoons honey
- 1 banana

DIRECTIONS

1. **In a blender place all ingredients and blend until smooth**
2. **Pour smoothie in a glass and serve**

KALE SMOOTHIE

Serves: *1*
Prep Time: 5   Minutes
Cook Time: 5   Minutes
Total Time: *10* Minutes

INGREDIENTS

- 1 cup kale leaves
- 1 cup vanilla yogurt
- 1 cup soy milk
- 1 cup pineapple pieces
- 1 tsp honey

DIRECTIONS

1. In a blender place all ingredients and blend until smooth
2. Pour smoothie in a glass and serve

CARROT SMOOTHIE

Serves: *1*

Prep Time: 5   Minutes

Cook Time: 5   Minutes

Total Time: *10*   Minutes

INGREDIENTS

- 2 carrots
- 1 apple
- 1 cup celery
- 1 cup coconut water

DIRECTIONS

1. In a blender place all ingredients and blend until smooth
2. Pour smoothie in a glass and serve

Serves: **1**

Prep Time: **5**   Minutes

Cook Time: **5**   Minutes

Total Time: **10** Minutes

INGREDIENTS

- 1 banana
- 1 cup cherries
- 1 cup spinach
- 1 cup almond milk
- 1 cup ice

DIRECTIONS

1. In a blender place all ingredients and blend until smooth
2. Pour smoothie in a glass and serve

AVOCADO SMOOTHIE

Serves: *1*
Prep Time: 5   Minutes

Cook Time: 5   Minutes

Total Time: *10* Minutes

INGREDIENTS

- 1 cup blueberries
- 1 cup spinach
- 1 avocado
- 1 tablespoon chia seeds
- 1 tsp honey

DIRECTIONS

1. In a blender place all ingredients and blend until smooth
2. Pour smoothie in a glass and serve

CRANBERRY SMOOTHIE

Serves: *1*
Prep Time: *5*   Minutes

Cook Time: *5*   Minutes

Total Time: *10* Minutes

INGREDIENTS

- 1 cup cranberries
- 1 apple
- 1 banana
- 1 handful baby spinach
- 1 cup cranberry juice

DIRECTIONS

1. In a blender place all ingredients and blend until smooth
2. Pour smoothie in a glass and serve

Serves: *1*
Prep Time: 5   Minutes

Cook Time: 5   Minutes

Total Time: *10*   Minutes

INGREDIENTS

- 1 banana
- 1 avocado
- 3 oz. spinach
- 1 mango
- 1 cup grapes
- 1 cup coconut water

DIRECTIONS

1. In a blender place all ingredients and blend until smooth
2. Pour smoothie in a glass and serve

THANK YOU FOR READING THIS BOOK!

CPSIA information can be obtained
at www.ICGtesting.com
Printed in the USA
BVHW031236300520
580600BV00004B/42